DRILL TEAM
is for me

Valerie Childress
and Jane Nelson

photographs by
David Peterson

Lerner Publications Company   Minneapolis

The authors wish to thank Nan Nowlin and the Marcus High School Marquettes and Kay Rushing and the Lewisville High School Farmerettes.

Additional photographs courtesy of Marcus (Texas) High School and the Lewisville (Texas) *Daily Leader*
Photograph on page 32 (bottom) by Sidney Eads

*To our families, and to all girls across the country
who have and who will participate in drill team*

LIBRARY OF CONGRESS CATALOGING IN PUBLICATION DATA

Childress, Valerie.
    Drill team is for me.

    Summary: Text and photographs follow a member of a drill team as she learns the basic commands and leg moves and progresses to more complicated marching and show routines for her first public performance.
    1. Drill (not military)—Juvenile literature.
[1. Drill (not military)]   I. Nelson, Jane.
II. Peterson, David, ill. III. Title.
GV1797.C73   1986   791   85-19737
ISBN 0-8225-1148-7 (lib. bdg.)

Manufactured in the United States of America

International Standard Book Number: 0-8225-1148-7
Library of Congress Catalog Card Number: 85-19737

2 3 4 5 6 7 8 9 10 94 93 92 91 90 89 88 87

Hello! My name is Alison. My favorite
sport is drill team, and I'd like to tell you
about it. Drill team is a team sport that
puts together snappy and precise marching
movements to make routines. You match
your movements to the beat of music and
to the movement of the other members of
the team. My team is called the Marching
Missies, and I became a member last year.

I first became interested in drill team after spending a weekend with my friend Casey. Casey's older sister, Kristi, is a member of the Marcus High School Marquettes drill team, and she was getting ready to perform in a show at the school gym. I really enjoyed watching Kristi perform. She looked like she was having so much fun. And she looked so pretty in her uniform.

Later that night, I asked Kristi how I could become a member of a drill team. She told me about the Marching Missies, a program for young girls that was sponsored by the community education department. Kristi was an assistant to the director, and she promised to help me sign up for the team.

I could hardly wait to ask my parents about joining the drill team. Mom and Dad were interested, but they wanted to find out more about the program. So Kristi introduced Mom and me to Ms. Nelson, the director of the Marching Missies.

Ms. Nelson told us that drill team offers its members the opportunity to develop poise and physical fitness and to learn team work. She said that the program also gives girls a chance to meet new friends and to perform in the community.

5

"Although some of the girls find drill easier if they have studied dance, don't worry if you have not taken dance lessons before," said Ms. Nelson. "You can become a good drill team member if you can count and if you are willing to work hard."

Ms. Nelson told us that joining a drill team didn't have to be expensive. Regular

play clothes that had plenty of stretch were perfect for practice. Ms. Nelson suggested that we wear leotards and tights, shorts and knit shirts, or sweat suits. We also had to wear tennis shoes and socks. Special costumes would be required for performances, but many parents saved money by making the outfits.

Ms. Nelson then told us about three kinds of drill team performances: **parades, field shows** at sporting events, and **special event shows.** The Marching Missies would work in all three areas. The team had already received invitations to perform in the opening ceremony at the Rodeo and Fat Stock Show and to march in the Rodeo Parade. The rodeo was only four weeks away, and Ms. Nelson said that everyone would have to work extra hard to learn a show and a parade routine in such a short time.

7

I was really excited when I heard about the parade and the show, and Mom was pleased with Ms. Nelson's program, too. I signed up for the Marching Missies that day. Casey also signed up, and we were impatient to begin practice.

At our first workout, Kristi showed us how to fix our hair so it would not be in our faces while we performed. She said that once practice started, we would be concentrating on our routines and wouldn't have time to worry about our appearance. She also told us that jewelry was not allowed because it could catch on our clothes and might cause an injury.

When everyone was ready, we began to warm up with stretching exercises. Ms. Nelson told us that stretching before working out was important and would prevent pulled muscles and sprains and help to tone our muscles. She reminded us to breathe deeply while we stretched so our bodies would take in plenty of oxygen.

One of our favorite exercises stretched almost every part of the body. We began by sitting on the floor with our backs straight, hands on knees, and legs and toes pointed forward. We bent our feet at the ankles, pointing our toes to the sky, and then stretched them forward again. After doing this eight times, we stretched our arms up

and slowly lowered them to our sides. We did this four times. Then we lifted our shoulders to our ears four times. Finally, we did circles with our legs, arms, shoulders, and head.

We did other exercises to build strength in our legs, arms, and stomach. Our work-out included sit-ups, jumping jacks, leg lifts, and flutter kicks.

Good posture is very important in drill team. Ms. Nelson said that good posture shows that you have pride in yourself and in your team. To check your posture, stand sideways in front of a mirror and see if your chin is level, your shoulders straight, your stomach in, and your hips tucked. This is called **mirroring**.

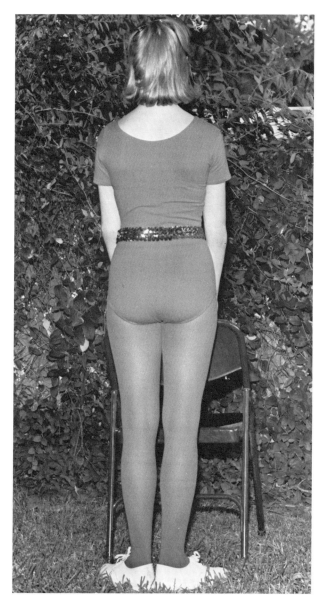
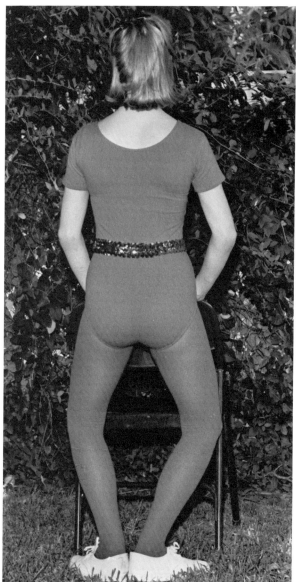

A good exercise for improving posture is the **plié**, a ballet movement. Stand up straight and hold the back of a chair with both hands. Put your feet in a V-shape on the floor. Lower your body slowly by bending only your knees and ankles. Then straighten up. Repeat this exercise eight times.

After we warmed up. we began to learn some of the basic drill **commands**. There are two types of commands, **standing** and **marching**. Standing commands are performed while you are standing in a fixed position, and marching commands are done while you are moving forward.

In order to help everybody do the same movements at the same time, we use a counting system. Each movement is broken into parts, and each part is performed on the count of one, two, three, and so on. You really have to concentrate on keeping count, or you can easily fall out of step.

Kristi and Ms. Nelson showed us the standing commands first. **Attention** is the starting position for each routine. On the count of one, move your left foot to your right foot, placing the arch of the left foot behind the heel of the right foot. Place your hands on your hip bones with fingers together and wrists straight. On the count of two, snap your head up to attention.

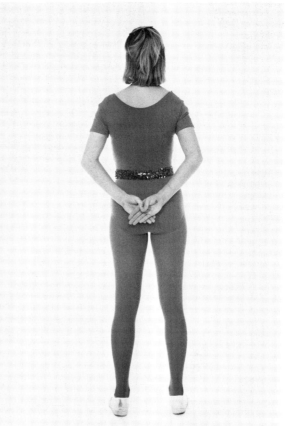

At ease is a command that allows you to hold your place in a more relaxed manner. This command is usually given from the attention position. When you hear the "at ease" command, you can move your left foot, but your right foot must remain in place. Move the left foot until your feet are parallel and a comfortable distance apart. Clasp your left hand in the right hand behind your back. Hold your shoulder back and your head up, and remember that no talking is allowed!

Right face is a one-quarter turn from a position of attention. On the count of one, put your left foot in front of your body. On the count of two, make a quarter turn to the right, using the balls of your feet as pivots. On the count of three, pull your left foot to the right foot in the attention position. Your head should face front until the third count when it snaps one-quarter turn to face the new direction. **Left face** is the opposite of right face.

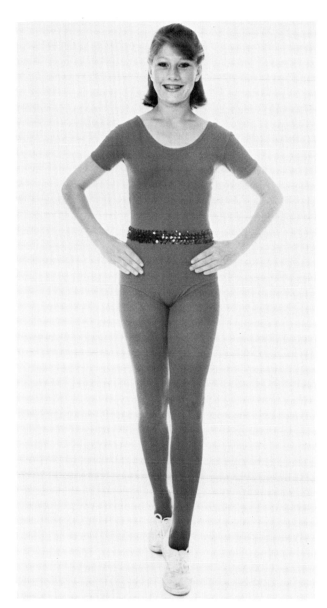

About face is a one-half turn performed from the attention position. On the count of one, place the ball of your left foot in front of your body. On the count of two, go up to the balls of both feet and pivot to face the opposite direction. The head moves with the body. On the count of three, pull your left foot to the right foot and assume the attention position.

Mark time is the command to march in place. Marking time begins from the attention position. Keeping your toes pointed down, lift your left foot to the level of your right knee. Your toes should leave the ground last. Lower your left foot to the ground and count one. Next, lift your right foot in the same manner and lower it to the ground on the count of two. Continue marking time until the "halt!" command is given.

Halt is the command to stop. After you hear, "Ready, halt!" take two more steps. On the count of one, your left foot strikes the ground. On the count of two, you take a step with the right foot. On the count of three, place the left foot against the right in the attention position. Your head should also snap up to attention on the third count.

Marching is a forward motion begun after the command, "Ready, march!" Always begin marching with your left foot and use the same leg and foot positions as in marking time.

One of the hardest part of marching as a team is keeping the lines straight. Always line yourself up with two team members—the person on the far right in your horizontal row and the first person in your vertical row. Sometimes Ms. Nelson

would call "**Dress right**" to help us get the lines straight. When you hear, "Dress right," turn your head and eyes to the right. **Dress front** is the command telling you to snap your head back to face the front.

The basic commands are put together in many different combinations to make **routines**. I worked hard to learn the commands and practiced by myself at home.

But even after I had learned the commands, I had to put in many more hours of practice with the team. Because drill teams are viewed as a unit, the group's movements are more important than any one member's. At first, it was hard to stay together, but the more we practiced together, the easier it became.

I quickly learned there was more to think about than just the commands. As our routines became more familiar, we began to concentrate on **showmanship**. Showmanship is projecting your energy and personality to the audience. Snappy movements, popular music, and variety can help to make your performance more appealing.

Something as simple as smiling, for instance, will make your team more attractive. Ms. Nelson said that the highest kicks and the smartest routines are even better when they are done with glowing smiles. To encourage us to smile, a trophy is awarded to the girl who has the best continuous smile during each parade or show.

To look our very best, Ms. Nelson encouraged us to exercise and to get plenty of sleep, eat healthy foods, and drink lots of water. A healthy body looks good, and it also has greater stamina for long parades and fast-paced shows.

Costumes and uniforms add color to drill team performances. Uniforms should be in good taste and fit well, and they should be stretchy enough to allow you to perform kicks, bends, and movements comfortably. You don't have to spend a lot of money to have a showy uniform, either.

By adding accessories such as sequin belts, bib overlays, or trim, you can change one basic leotard and skirt into several different costumes. Most teams wear white tennis shoes and white socks, but some drill teams wear leather boots instead.

Props also add color and drama to performances. Props are objects like umbrellas, beach balls, ladders, stools, hoops, or flashlights that become part of your routine. Pom poms and colored gloves are the most popular props, but you can use just about anything if you are creative.

You can select your show music from among many types of music. Some drill teams perform with live bands, but most teams perform to recorded music. Instrumental music is usually more successful than songs with words, and popular tunes are always fun to use.

Listen to the music that you have chosen. You will notice that all music can be broken down into sections of eight beats. Your routines will be built around movements measured in eight counts to fit the music. If the song is fast, your movements will be fast. If your music is slow, your routine will be counted slowly to match the beat.

Like most drill teams, the Marching Missies used a lot of **leg work** in their routines. Leg work includes kicks, leg lifts, knee lifts, and splits. After practicing them. I understood why leg exercises were so important!

At first, kick only as high as you comfortably can so that you don't injure yourself. With practice and regular stretching, your kicks will reach eye level or higher. It is important that you keep your back straight when you kick.

To do a **jump kick**, jump on your left foot while you kick your right foot straight forward. Remember to keep your toes pointed and your right leg straight. Your left leg should be straight, but do not lock your knee. Keep your left heel slightly off the ground. After you drop your right leg, take a jump on your right foot and kick your left leg in the same way.

Leg lifts from a standing position do not involve jumping. One leg is held straight with the foot flat on the ground while the other leg is lifted to knee, waist, or eye level. Leg lifts look very pretty when you change legs and do several in a row.

Knee lifts are similar to leg lifts except that you bend your knee and point your toes down. Lift your foot to knee level.

The **splits** must be learned gradually, and you should always warm up with stretching exercises before trying them. To do the splits, point your leading toe forward and slide your legs apart. Keep your back straight and your head up. Your hand positions can vary according to the routine. They may be in an attention position, held out to the sides, or rested at your sides.

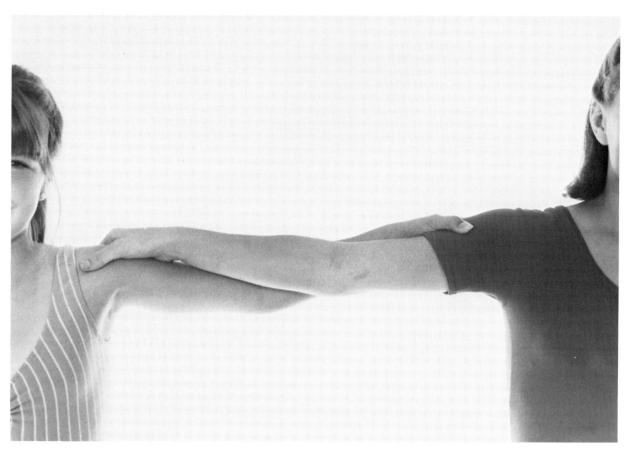

If you are doing leg work by yourself, keep your hands in an attention position. If leg work is part of a team routine, the members will often interlock their arms. This is called **locking**. To lock arms, lift your left arm and lightly place your hand on the shoulder of the person to your left. Then lift your right arm and place it on the shoulder of the girl to your right. The persons at the ends of the lines should place their free hands on their hips in the attention position.

For wider spacing, you may lock with your hands lightly grasping the elbow of your neighbor. But regardless of the method of locking, you should not put your weight on someone else. Everyone must carry her own weight. If you pull down on the girl next to you, you will hurt her performance.

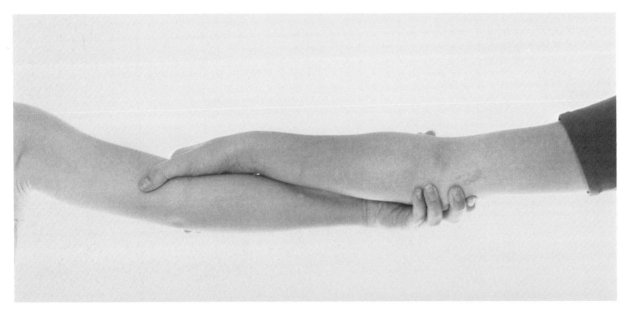

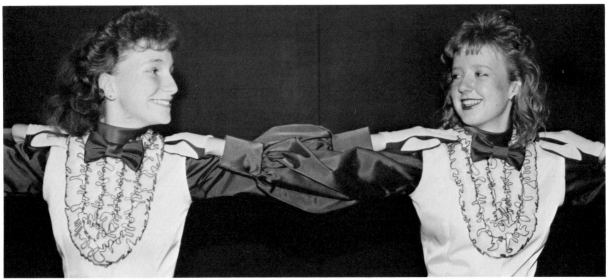

Sometimes we practiced movements with pom poms so we did not have to concentrate so much on hand positions. When we practiced without pom poms, we held four fingers together with thumbs out and wrists straight. When our arms were overhead, we turned our hands so that the palms faced each other. When our arms were held straight out, our palms faced down.

We learned a routine with pom poms for the opening show of the rodeo. The routine was to be performed in 72 counts. My favorite part was a **contagion**. A contagion gives a ripple or wave effect to group movement. The wave is created when each girl performs her moves a fraction of a second after the girl in front of her. Ms. Nelson calls the contagion a crowd pleaser because everyone enjoys watching it.

COUNT	MOVEMENT
1-3	Face rear in attention position.
4	Drop both arms down to sides.
5-8	About face. On the count of 5, raise right arm in front of you. On 6, lift arm overhead. On 7, drop arm to side. On 8, pull both hands into attention position at the waist. This move can be done as a contagion.
1-8	March forward eight steps.

1-2-3 4 5-6

7 8 1-2-3-4 5-6-7-8

COUNT	MOVEMENT
1-8	On the count of **1**, step at an angle to the left. On **2**, do right knee lift. On **3**, bring feet together. On **4**, do right leg lift. On **5**, step down on right foot. Facing front on the count of **6**, march on left foot. At the same time, swing right arm full circle in a clockwise direction. On **7**, march on right foot. On **8**, march on left foot and stop arm movement with hand extended out to the right side.

COUNT	MOVEMENT
1-8	On the count of **1**, angle to the right. On **2**, do a left knee lift. On **3**, bring feet together. On **4**, do a left leg lift. On **5**, step down on left foot. Facing front on **6**, swing left arm in full circle counter-clockwise. March on right foot. On **7**, march on left foot. On the count of **8**, bring your feet together and assume the attention position (see page 38).

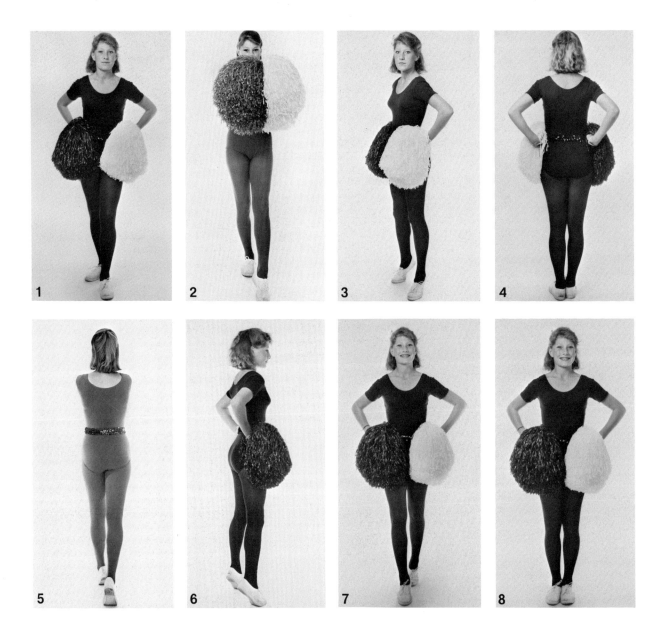

COUNT	MOVEMENT
1-8	About face. On the count of 1, push both pom poms out in front. On 2 and 3, return pom poms to the waist. On 4, hold at attention. On the count of 5, push the pom poms behind you. On 6 and 7, about face and hold pom poms at waist. On 8, hold at attention.

COUNT	MOVEMENT
1-8	On 1, bend both knees in a squat position and place left hand on the floor. On 2, place right hand on the floor. On 3, stand and bring left hand to waist. On 4, bring right hand to waist. On 5, lift left hand straight overhead. On 6, raise right hand overhead. On 7, bring left hand to waist. On 8, bring right hand to waist.

COUNT	MOVEMENT
1-8	Repeat last eight counts, leaving pom poms on the floor after the first and second counts (see page 39).
1-4	Beginning with left foot, march backward.
5-8	On the counts of 5 and 6, lock left arm. Lock right arm on 7 and 8.
1-8	Do eight kick jumps, dropping arms to side with feet together. End routine in contagion splits. Put your left hand on the floor at your side with your right hand straight overhead.

We practiced very hard to learn our parade routine, too. The routine was a short one that could be repeated as we marched forward in the parade. The entire routine was performed in 48 counts, but it was easier to remember the moves in six groups of eight counts. Here is our parade routine:

COUNT	MOVEMENT
1-8	Beginning with the left foot, take eight marching steps.
1-4	On the count of **1**, drop right hand straight down. Count **2-4**, draw a full circle in a clockwise direction, holding arm straight. End with right arm straight down on **4**. Follow hand movement with head.

5-8 On count of **5**, drop left hand straight down. Counts **6-8**, draw a full circle counter-clockwise, holding arm straight. End with left arm straight down.

1-4 On counts **1-3**, march three steps. Swing arm straight out as opposite leg lifts up. On **4**, pull left arm behind you. Head looks back toward left hand. Right arm is held out front.

5-8 Fan: On counts **5** and **6**, pull both hands together overhead and bring them to chest level. On counts **7** and **8**, pull hands apart overhead. This time, the left arm is held out front and the right arm is held back. Face left on all four counts.

1-2-3-4-5-6-7-8

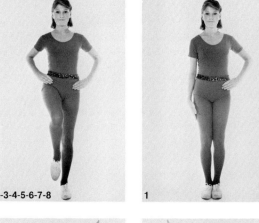
1

2

3

4

5-6

7-8

1-2-3

4

5-6

7

8

1-6	Lift left arm overhead to front. This can be done by rows as a contagion, one count per row.
7-8	Pull both arms in to waist.
1-4	On the count of **1**, bring left hand to left shoulder. On **2**, raise hand straight overhead. Hold on **3**, and lower hand to waist on **4**.
5-8	On the count of **5**, bring right hand to left shoulder. On **6** and **7**, raise right hand straight overhead. On **8**, lower hand to waist.
1-4	On the count of **1**, bring both hands shoulder height with elbows out. On **2** and **3**, raise hands straight overhead. On **4**, lower hands to waist.
5-8	End with four marching steps.

1-2-3-4-5-6

7

8

1

2-3

4

5

6-7

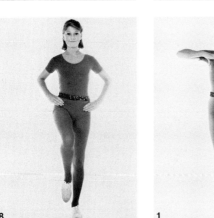

8

1

2-3

4-5-6-7-8

Everyone helped each other to get ready for our rodeo parade. We checked our hair and costumes, and Kristi showed us how to apply stage make-up. We wore red lipstick and dark eye make-up so our eyes and mouths could be seen from a distance. I had never performed in public before, so I was excited and a little nervous, too. I took a deep breath as we started to march.

All of our practice paid off. No one missed a step during the entire parade. The spectators clapped and enjoyed our routines. After the parade, friends and relatives gathered around to congratulate us. Kristi hugged Casey and me and told us that we looked as good as her high school drill team! Ms. Nelson said we did a great job and that she was very proud of us. I felt really good.

I felt even happier when Ms. Nelson called my name as the winner of the smile trophy! I was having so much fun, and I still had our show performance to look forward to. I'm so glad that I became a drill team member, and I hope you'll think about joining a drill team, too.

DRILL TEAM Words

ABOUT FACE: A one-half turn from the attention position

AT EASE: A more relaxed standing position than standing at attention

ATTENTION: The starting position for every routine

COMMAND: An order given by the director to tell the team what move to perform

CONTAGION: A wave-like group movement that happens when each team member begins her move a fraction of a second after the girl standing in front of her

DIRECTOR: The person who teaches and directs a drill team

DRESS FRONT: To face the front after having faced the side

DRESS RIGHT: To look to the right

FIELD PERFORMANCE: A show performed at an outdoor sporting event

FLEXIBILITY: The ability to stretch and move muscles easily

FULL EXTENSION: To stretch an arm or leg without bending at the joints

HALT: To stop marking time or marching forward

JUMP KICK: A kick preceded by a small jump or bounce

KNEE LIFT: To lift the knee waist high while holding the toes pointed down

LEFT FACE: A one-quarter turn to the left from the attention position

LEG LIFT: A straight leg kick with toe pointed

LOCKING: The interlocking of arms with other drill team members

MARCH: To move forward in measured steps, starting with the left foot

MARK TIME: To march in place

MIRRORING: To check posture in front of a mirror

PLIÉ: A knee bend exercise used to improve posture

POSTURE: The way the body is held

PROP: An object such as a hoop or ladder used in a show

RIGHT FACE: A one-quarter turn to the right from the attention position

ROUTINE: A group of movements put together in a special order

SHOWMANSHIP: To project energy and personality to an audience through a performance

STAGE MAKE-UP: The heavier-than-normal make-up worn for a performance

ABOUT THE AUTHORS AND THE PHOTOGRAPHER

VALERIE CHILDRESS' interest and involvement in drill team is a result of her daughter's participation in both high school and college drill team. Childress is an educator, librarian, and freelance writer, and her feature articles have appeared in many magazines and newspapers.

JANE NELSON, a graduate of North Texas State University, has taught hundreds of drill team and baton twirling students over the past 20 years. She is a member of several professional organizations, including the Drill Team Directors of America.

DAVID PETERSON is a member of The Professional Photographers of America, the Southwestern Professional Photographers, the Texas Professional Photographers Association, and Wedding Photographers International. He owns his own photography studio and has won numerous awards for his work.